ENVIRONMENTAL PROTECTION AGENCY

AGENTS OF GOVERNMENT

Published by Creative Education and Creative Paperbacks
P.O. Box 227, Mankato, Minnesota 56002
Creative Education and Creative Paperbacks are
imprints of The Creative Company
www.thecreativecompany.us

Design and production by Chelsey Luther
Art direction by Rita Marshall

Printed in Malaysia

Photographs by Alamy (Stock Connection Blue), Corbis (AP, Bettmann, Carlos Cazalis, W.
Cody, Patrick J. Endres/AlaskaPhotoGraphics, SEAN GARDNER/Reuters, Chris Henderson,
Talia Herman, Andrew Holbrooke, Andrew Lichtenstein, Reuters), deviantART (AllydNYC),
Dreamstime (Alexey Rozhanovsky, Tinnaporn Sàthapornnanont, Olivér Svéd), Flickr
(Mark Ho), Getty Images (Fox Photos, Fred G. Korth/Stringer, Santi Visalli), iStockphoto
(ericfoltz), Shutterstock (anweber, Danicek, Nneirda, Paul Stringer), Wisconsin Historical
Society

Library of Congress Cataloging-in-Publication Data
Wimmer, Teresa.
Environmental Protection Agency / Teresa Wimmer.
p. cm. — (Agents of government)
Summary: An in-depth look at the people and policies behind the government agency known
as the EPA, from its founding in 1970 to the controversies and challenges it faces today.
Includes bibliographical references and index.

ISBN 978-1-60818-544-3 (hardcover)
ISBN 978-1-62832-145-6 (pbk)

1. United States. Environmental Protection Agency—Juvenile literature. 2. Environmental protection—United States—Juvenile literature. 3. Environmental disasters—Juvenile literature.
I. Title.

TABLE OF CONTENTS

It may be hard to believe, but before 1970, a factory could spew black clouds of toxic chemicals into the air, filling the city air with haze,

or dump **hazardous waste** into lakes and rivers, coating them with sludge. And it was all perfectly legal. Companies were rarely convicted and ordered to stop such behaviors. There was no agency or law in place to prevent people from endangering the environment, and there were no punishments, either. In December 1970, the United States Senate confirmed president Richard Nixon's choice of an administrator for a new federal agency to tackle environmental issues. In the words of the U.S. Environmental Protection Agency (EPA), its purpose is "to ensure that all Americans are protected from significant risks to human health and the environment where they live, learn, and work." The EPA coordinates and supports research and antipollution activities conducted by state and local governments, private and public groups, individuals, and educational institutions. Without the EPA, there would be no legal way to limit or eliminate pollution to air, water, and land, and all life on Earth could be in jeopardy.

In the late 1800s, pollution from factories in industrial cities such as Pittsburgh, Pennsylvania, filled the air.

A Dirty World

Notions of environmental responsibility existed centuries before the EPA was created. As early as 1652, when the U.S. was still a collection of colonies, the city of Boston established a public water supply to provide clean water to its citizens. Other large cities then followed its example. Throughout the 18th and 19th centuries, as more people settled in the U.S., the negative effects of having large populations occupy relatively small areas became more apparent. Sewage often lined city streets and floated into rivers and the ocean, and drinking water was often mixed with sediment and other contaminants.

The rapid **industrialization** that occurred in the late 19th century only added to the environmental pollution. Factory smokestacks blew chemical-heavy soot into the air. Industrial waste and oil floated in waterways. By the 1860s, some people had become concerned about the harm being done to the environment. A new **conservation** movement was born. In 1872, geologist Ferdinand Hayden convinced Congress to make Yellowstone a national park. The founding of Yellowstone began a worldwide national

Conservationists became worried that wild places such as the Grand Canyon would be ruined by human activity.

park movement. Leading the way was naturalist and photographer John Muir, whose work in Yosemite helped Congress preserve that area as a national park in 1890. Other activists included 26th U.S. president Theodore Roosevelt, who set aside 5 wilderness areas to be designated as national parks in the early 1900s.

No amount of land conservation could protect the world against the poisons introduced during World War I (1914–18), though. Chemicals such as chlorine, phosgene, and mustard gas were inhaled by soldiers and coated their lungs, sometimes leading to blindness and death. Other new chemicals such as pesticides and nitrates were used to fertilize crops. And substances such as benzene (in automobile gasoline) and asbestos (in many building materials) were used in manufacturing. Few laws existed to protect the environment and people from toxins. Through the years, such chemicals accumulated and drained into the groundwater, lakes, rivers, and oceans, and even evaporated into the air.

In the 1930s, a large portion of the Great Plains region became known as the Dust Bowl during a period of severe drought and fierce dust storms. Dry conditions and years of poor farming methods on the prairie caused loose soil to blow away in sky-blackening clouds. People developed respiratory, or breathing, problems from being exposed to so many fine particles of dust. In 1933, president Franklin Roosevelt's "New Deal" created programs to assist farmers and conserve the nation's natural resources, among other things. The Soil Conservation Service, founded in 1935, later applied scientific practices and taught farmers new plowing techniques to reduce soil erosion. In 1937, the Pittman–Robertson Act was signed, establishing a permanent fund for states' fish and wildlife programs. The fund was based upon money gained from federal taxes on hunting and fishing equipment and ammunition.

American involvement in World War II in the 1940s brought about the development—and use—of **nuclear** weapons. With the bombing of the Japanese cities of Hiroshima and Nagasaki in August 1945, a new type of destructive power was unleashed. Apart from the thousands of

Few laws existed to protect the environment and people from toxins.

During the eight-year drought in the Dust Bowl, dirt covered everything and could swallow up buildings and cars.

In 1950s Los Angeles, smog could make daytime seem like night, and the traffic only made matters worse.

people killed, plant and animal life in those areas were also affected. Media stories covered the **radioactive** fallout and its effect on food chains. The concept of **ecology** took on increased importance for people.

After the war, the U.S. population grew, and many people spread out beyond big cities to suburban areas. They thought they would leave behind problems associated with city sewage smells and pollution. However, the increased land development brought up new issues of waste treatment and natural resource depletion. New chemicals intended to make life easier, such as those found in lawn fertilizer and household cleaning materials, hit the market. These chemicals would eventually further contaminate the groundwater.

Oceans had also become dirtier by midcentury. People were advised against eating certain fish because they contained high concentrations of mercury, a chemical that can be dangerous to the human brain and nervous system. In many parts of the country, tap water was no longer considered safe for people to drink because of its high chemical content. To help combat water pollution, Congress passed the Federal Water Pollution Control Act (FWPCA) in 1948, which established a national policy for the prevention and control of water pollution. It opened the door for further water-protection legislation.

As water sources received greater attention, though, people neglected what was happening to air quality. Use of automobiles exploded during the 1950s, and more cars on the road meant more gaseous fumes in the air. More people began to be diagnosed with asthma and other breathing difficulties. The Air Pollution Control Act—the first federal law dealing with air pollution in the U.S.—was passed in 1955 because of several alarming problems, including a thick blanket of **smog** that covered Los Angeles, California. In 1952, a "fog" of pollution crossed the Atlantic Ocean from London, killing more than 4,000 people over a 4-day period.

In the 1960s, a powerful new wave of activism swept across the country and much of the world. Marches promoting civil rights for racial minorities and women took place in many U.S.

Congress passed the ... FWPCA in 1948, which established a national policy for the prevention and control of water pollution.

cities. People began to question the wisdom of some authority figures and laws, and policies concerning the environment were no exception. This environmental movement was inspired by Rachel Carson's 1962 book *Silent Spring*, which detailed the use of pesticides and their widespread, poisonous effect on humans and nature. The book sparked a public outcry for the federal government to protect natural lands from further pollution. *Silent Spring* helped to launch the concept of environmentalism as we know it today—a political movement that demands both government-sponsored preservation of the earth and consequences for those who pollute it. During the

1960s, presidents John F. Kennedy and Lyndon B. Johnson took note of this concern and added the environment to their list of campaign issues.

When president Richard Nixon took office in 1969, he expanded the federal government's role in protecting the environment with a series of new acts and programs. Congress paved the way for the first major federal environmental agency by passing the National Environmental Policy Act (NEPA), which Nixon signed into law on January 1, 1970. This act transformed the role of the federal government from mere conservator to lead protector. The law declared the government's intent to "assure for all

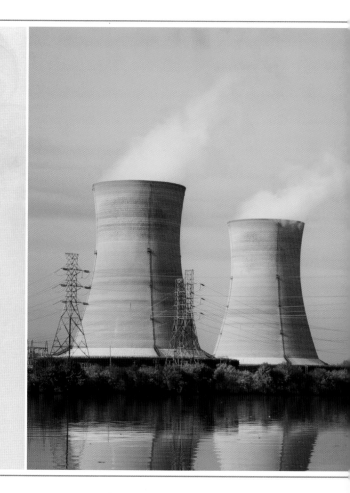

AGENCY INSIDER

THREE MILE ISLAND

On March 28, 1979, mechanical, electrical, and human errors led to a severe meltdown at Pennsylvania's Three Mile Island nuclear power plant. EPA officials arrived later that day and found that the accident was not as bad as feared, since radioactive material was kept to the containment building. Studies concluded that the amount of radiation people were exposed to was minimal. However, fears about the potential long-term risks to human health persist, decades later.

After Kennedy's death in 1963, Johnson carried on with both the presidency and their shared environmental policies.

Americans safe, healthful, productive, and aesthetically and culturally pleasing surroundings." From that point on, all federal agencies planning projects that would impact the environment in any way had to submit reports describing the possible consequences.

On February 10, 1970, Nixon asked Congress for $4 billion to improve water treatment facilities throughout the country. He also asked for national air quality standards and guidelines to decrease automobile emissions. Later, Nixon called for legislation to end the dumping of hazardous waste into the Great Lakes and proposed a plan to tighten standards for oil transportation by water. In 1973, he approved revisions to the National Oil and Hazardous Substances Pollution Contingency Plan, which had first been adopted in 1968.

On April 22, 1970, the first Earth Day celebration brought 20 million Americans out into the spring sunshine for peaceful demonstrations in favor of environmental reform. The success of Earth Day made federal legislation to protect the environment more important than ever. It also strengthened the idea that an independent federal agency was needed to coordinate all environmental protection and antipollution programs. On December 2, 1970, the Environmental Protection Agency was born with the confirmation of William Ruckelshaus as administrator, and the battle against environmental pollution officially began.

New Yorkers attended rallies and gathered peacefully for the first Earth Day on streets normally clogged with vehicles.

CHERNOBYL
Ukraine

The Chernobyl disaster occurred on April 26, 1986, when operators in the control room of the nuclear power plant's Reactor 4 botched a routine electrical experiment, resulting in an explosion that killed 2 and a fire that burned for 10 days. The radioactive fallout spread over 77,000 square miles (199,430 sq km) around the Ukrainian plant, driving more than a quarter of a million people from their homes. Radiation poisoning from the accident killed 28 people. Chernobyl remains the world's worst nuclear disaster to date.

Cleaning Up America

At least 13 different environmental programs from various federal offices were combined to form the EPA. This often led to power struggles among EPA officials, and the agency's early organizational structure was confusing. In time, though, the EPA came to administer 12 major federal environmental **statutes**, including the following: the Clean Air Act; the Clean Water Act; the Comprehensive Environmental Response, Compensation, and Liability Act (CERCLA, or Superfund); the Marine Protection, Research, and Sanctuaries Act; the Resource Conservation and Recovery Act (RCRA); the Federal Insecticide, Fungicide, and Rodenticide Act; the Toxic Substances Control Act; and the Safe Drinking Water Act.

One of the most influential initiatives of the EPA's early years was the Clean Air Act, which President Nixon signed on December 31, 1970. The act authorized the EPA to establish national air quality standards to protect public health and the environment from **greenhouse gas** emissions. Smog had become a major health concern in many American cities. The EPA wanted to limit the amount of factory emissions,

Once standards were put in place, air quality improved drastically throughout the 1970s in cities such as Chicago.

car exhaust, and paint solvents going into the air to keep them from being "cooked" by the sun and creating smog. The act also classified areas as "nonattainment areas" or "attainment areas," according to whether air quality fell short of or met the new national standards.

In a 1990 amendment, or change, to the Clean Air Act, the EPA was required to work with state governors to rank nonattainment areas. They used a scale of one (light) to five (extreme). The states then took responsibility for cleaning up any nonattainment areas. The amendment also instituted a program that required companies to obtain a permit from the state before releasing toxic chemicals into the air. Businesses paid permit fees, which funded the air pollution control activities. The 1990 amendment also tackled the nationwide **acid rain** problem. It set a permanent cap, or limit, on the total amount of sulfur dioxide and nitrogen oxide—contributors to acid rain—that electric power plants could emit. These restrictions helped reduce emissions to 7 million tons (6.4 million t) by 2005, or 41 percent below 1980 levels. In 2005, the EPA issued the Clean Air Interstate Rule, which set even

In 1972, the EPA addressed the problem of water pollution with the Clean Water Act ...

stricter caps on emissions from power plants in the eastern U.S. These efforts helped to further reduce emissions to 3.3 million tons (3 million t) by 2012, or 68 percent below 2005 levels.

In 1972, the EPA addressed the problem of water pollution with the Clean Water Act—several amendments to the original 1948 FWPCA. The 1972 amendments had two main goals: eliminating the discharge of all pollutants into U.S. waters by 1985 and establishing water control standards for the protection of fish, shellfish, and wildlife by 1983. The 1972 Clean Water Act also introduced the use of the National Pollutant Discharge Elimination System Permit Program, which required any company—such as wastewater treatment plants, factories, and construction companies—producing chemicals that would contaminate any body of water to first obtain a permit. States issued the permits, but the EPA administered the guidelines.

One of the first pesticide control acts the EPA implemented was its 1972 ban of DDT. DDT was among the first chemicals to be used on a broad scale as a pesticide. Following World War II, it was promoted as the simple solution to agricultural insect problems. By the 1960s, it was

Those who worked with gases meant to kill insects and other pests were equipped with heavy-duty protective gear.

Despite the obvious dangers of pesticides, people were still employed to handpick strawberries in the 1990s.

DANGER • PELIGRO

DANGER • PELIGRO

PESTICIDE   PESTICIDA

DO NOT
ENTER   NO
                        ENTRAR
                        MBD

suspected to cause cancer and threaten wildlife, particularly birds such as bald eagles. Since the ban went into effect, the bald eagle population has rebounded. Agricultural usage of DDT was banned worldwide in 2001, with exceptions for use in controlling disease-carrying mosquitoes in Mexico, Southeast Asia, and parts of Africa.

Pesticide restriction was taken to a new level with the Food Quality Protection Act of 1996. The act fundamentally changed the way the EPA regulated pesticides. It included a qualification that the use of pesticides on food crops could not endanger human health or the environment. The act also set a level of allowable pesticides considered safe for food. The standards were to be periodically evaluated by the EPA as new scientific information became available.

As the U.S. population and industries grew throughout the 20th century, so did the problem of where to dispose of hazardous waste. The issue came to a head with the Love Canal incident of 1976. Partially dug to connect the upper and lower segments of New York's Niagara River, the canal was never completed and became a dump-

ing ground. From 1947 to 1953, Hooker Chemical Company buried thousands of tons of toxic chemicals at the site. The canal area was then filled with dirt and sold to the Niagara Falls Board of Education, which later built a school and homes there. In 1976, it was discovered that chemicals from the Love Canal site had been seeping into basements of area homes, causing illnesses and miscarriages. Additionally, toxic chemicals were being carried through the city's sewers and improperly discharged into the Niagara River. In 1978 and 1980, president Jimmy Carter declared 2 separate environmental emergencies, relocating more than 900 families from the area surrounding the canal. In 1982, the EPA signed a $7-million agreement with the state of New York to clean up the Love Canal site. By 2004, the decontaminated area was no longer a national priority, but it continued to be monitored.

As news broke about the Love Canal disaster in 1976, Congress passed the RCRA, giving the EPA the authority to control hazardous waste "from cradle to grave"—from its generation, transportation, treatment, and storage to its dis-

As the U.S. population and industries grew throughout the 20th century, so did the problem of where to dispose of hazardous waste.

posal. The EPA could also decide what substances are classified as hazardous waste. Citizens and industries alike continue to challenge the EPA on its broad definition of the term.

In 1980, the scope of RCRA was widened by the adoption of CERCLA (commonly known as Superfund). For the first time, a law held persons or companies legally responsible for the release of hazardous chemicals or the creation of hazardous waste sites. It also provided for federal funds to clean up abandoned sites when no responsible party could be identified. A 1986 amendment to Superfund stressed the importance of creating new technologies to assist in removing hazard-

ous waste. The amendment also expanded each state's involvement in cleaning up hazardous waste sites within its borders and increased the federal antipollution fund to $8.5 billion.

Although **fossil fuels** are not considered hazardous waste, accidents such as oil spills still have the potential to cause great harm to human, plant, and animal life. If an oil spill is not contained, it can spread through an area's **ecosystem** and affect the food chain. The EPA combatted such an issue on March 24, 1989, when the *Exxon Valdez* oil tanker spilled more than 11 million gallons (41,640 cu m) of oil into Alaska's Prince William Sound. The spill contri-

AGENCY INSIDER

WILLIAM DOYLE RUCKELSHAUS

William Doyle Ruckelshaus served as the first EPA administrator (1970–73) and served again from 1983 to 1985. He helped the new agency get organized and took action against major industrial polluters. Ruckelshaus was also instrumental in setting EPA policy on pollutants, air quality, and permits. Because of his consistent and honest record at the EPA, he was appointed acting director of the Federal Bureau of Investigation (FBI) in April 1973, during a period of FBI scandals, to reform that agency's image.

EPA hazmat teams focused on testing the potentially harmful substances left behind when factories were abandoned.

buted to the deaths of more than 250,000 birds, 2,800 sea otters, 300 seals, 250 bald eagles, and more than 20 killer whales. Alaskan residents who ate sea life from the contaminated water suffered health problems, even decades later. The waters were eventually cleaned, and the EPA recommended that Exxon use **bioremediation** to replenish the oil-contaminated soil. Despite such efforts, oil chemicals were detected in the soil near the site of the spill in the early 2000s. The EPA continued to grapple with developing new techniques for the safe transportation and disposal of toxic substances such as oil.

The worst oil spill in U.S. history occurred on April 20, 2010, when methane gas from an underwater well caused BP's *Deepwater Horizon* oil rig to explode in the Gulf of Mexico. The accident caused 210 million gallons (780,000 cu m) of oil to leak into the Gulf's waters for 87 days, polluting more than 125 miles (201 km) of Louisiana's shoreline. In addition to claiming the lives of 11 people and injuring many others, the accident killed more than 8,000 animals. BP was ordered to pay nearly $40 billion in fines, cleanup costs, and settlements as a result of the oil spill, with an additional $16 billion to be paid to the Clean Water Act. Despite the cleanup efforts of more than 30,000 people, pollution lingered in the area for years.

Pelicans that were rescued from their oil-coated breeding grounds in 2010 were washed with dish soap and relocated.

CUYAHOGA FIRES
Ohio, U.S.A.

Decades of industrial waste pollution caused Ohio's Cuyahoga River to ignite at least 13 times between 1868 and 1969. A 1912 fire killed five, while a 1952 fire resulted in $1.5 million in damage. After another fire in 1969, a story published by *TIME* magazine brought national attention to water pollution issues. This prompted a flurry of water pollution control activities such as the Clean Water Act and helped inspire the creation of the EPA and the Ohio Environmental Protection Agency.

Working Together for Earth

Because the EPA was established as part of the executive branch of the federal government, it does not answer directly to Congress. The independently run organization conducts its own research from its headquarters in Washington, D.C. The EPA administrator reports directly to the U.S. president. However, the legislative branch of the federal government controls the organizational structure of the EPA. The judicial branch determines whether EPA policies and procedures are legal, but the EPA employs its own lawyers. It is also bound by rules set up under NEPA and the U.S. Constitution.

The administrator is supported by a staff of 1 deputy, 3 associate, 12 assistant, and 10 regional administrators. The regional administrators head each of the EPA's 10 regional offices around the country. Regional offices act as liaisons between EPA headquarters and individual state environmental agencies and departments. The regional offices also assist with issuing permits and administering local programs and activities. They inform the public about which chemicals are used at individual facilities and

The EPA's Federal Triangle headquarters in D.C. strives to be as energy efficient and responsible as it can be.

released into the environment (known as the Community Right-to-Know provisions). At EPA headquarters are 12 sub-offices, including the offices of Administration and Resources Management, Chief Financial Officer, Enforcement and Compliance Assurance, Environmental Information, General Counsel, Inspector General, and International and Tribal Affairs. Another sub-office, the Office of Research and Development (ORD), coordinates with each of the four program-specific sub-offices: Air and Radiation, Chemical Safety and Pollution Prevention, Solid Waste and Emergency Response, and Water.

To hold a leadership position within the EPA, an individual must obtain a bachelor's degree or higher and have several years' experience in environmental quality control. Staff are highly educated and technically trained; more than half are engineers, scientists, and policy analysts. EPA administrator Gina McCarthy earned a bachelor's degree in social anthropology from the University of Massachusetts at Boston and a joint master of science in environmental health engineering and planning and policy from Tufts University. While serving as commissioner of the Connecticut Depart-

ment of Environmental Protection from 2004 to 2009, she implemented a regional policy to reduce greenhouse gas emissions from power plants. Because of her commitment to addressing issues related to climate change, president Barack Obama appointed her in 2009 as assistant administrator for the EPA's Office of Air and Radiation and then as its administrator in 2013.

To keep pace with the environmental policy demands of a changing world, the EPA's size has also expanded throughout the years, from a force of approximately 5,000 employees in 1970 to just under 16,000 by 2014. The EPA inherited 183 buildings at 84 sites in 26 states when it began. Of those sites, about half were research laboratories, many of which conducted duplicate research or had outdated equipment. In an effort to increase efficiency, the EPA consolidated them into 27 labs by the early 1980s. The growth of the EPA and the continuous updating of its lab equipment called for funding to increase, though. The EPA's budget went up $9 billion over the course of 40 years—reaching just under the $8-billion mark in 2013.

The Office of Administrative Law Judges

> *To keep pace with the environmental policy demands of a changing world, the EPA's size has also expanded …*

Still the most widespread
and relatively inexpensive
energy source, coal power
remains a troubling
polluter, too.

rchers at ORD
or the health
l ecosystems
elp of aerial
bhy.

(OALJ) is an independent office in the EPA's Office of Administration and Resources Management. If a company violates an environmental law enforced by the EPA, the EPA may take legal action. The OALJ then steps in to hear the case in court and make its verdict. Whenever possible, the four administrative law judges offer **mediation** to allow the company to correct its mistakes instead of going to court. If the company does not accept mediation and is found guilty, the EPA may issue a fine and force the company to bring its standards in line with the law. The OALJ also presides over permit cases to make sure companies that emit toxic chemicals into the air or water obtain the proper permit.

Sometimes the violating individual or business decides to take legal action against, or appeal, an OALJ decision. Then the Environmental Appeals Board (EAB) comes in. The EAB is a committee of four judges appointed by the administrator. Three out of the four are assigned to each case so that their decision can be made by majority vote. The EAB determines whether the OALJ ruling should be upheld. Eight attorneys

provide counsel to the EAB. They assist the EAB in analyzing laws and policies and preparing formal, written legal opinions. They also answer questions from the general public about the appeals process.

To ensure the EPA itself is abiding by federal law, the Office of the Inspector General (OIG), an EPA headquarters sub-office, holds the agency accountable. Although the OIG is a part of the EPA, it acts independently to audit (make financial inspections), evaluate, and investigate the EPA and its contractors each year to make sure funds are being used appropriately. Congress provides the OIG with its own funds to ensure the office is kept free from and unbiased toward the EPA. Twice per year, the OIG provides a report to Congress that identifies areas where the EPA can be made more efficient.

With an eye on populations to come, the EPA works constantly on futuristic technologies and looks for new ways to ensure the planet's safety. The EPA's headquarters sub-office ORD manages laboratories, research centers, and offices across the country. ORD scientists conduct lab

To ensure the EPA itself is abiding by federal law, the Office of the Inspector General ... holds the agency accountable.

tests to discover how chemicals harm humans and animals and develop new procedures for reducing their negative effects. The EPA's Clean Automotive Technology program researches alternative fuels, such as **biodiesel** and electricity, that would reduce greenhouse gas emissions. Its pump-and-treat system is a common method for cleaning up contaminated groundwater. In such a system, groundwater is pumped from wells to an aboveground treatment system that removes such contaminants as industrial solvents, metals, and fuel oil. The pumping action helps keep contaminants from reaching drinking water wells, wetlands, streams, and other natural resources. To reduce pollution and improve air quality, in 2013, the EPA set aside $2 million for rebates to help construction equipment owners replace or update older diesel engines.

Since 1995, the EPA's Brownfields Program has changed the way contaminated property is dealt with and managed. A brownfield is land that was once contaminated and still may contain low levels of hazardous materials but has the potential to be reused. Land that is more severely contaminated and has high concentrations of hazardous waste or pollution, such as a Superfund site, cannot be categorized as a brownfield. The EPA provides grant money, or

AGENCY INSIDER

SUPERFUND

With the Comprehensive Environmental Response, Compensation, and Liability Act of 1980, "Superfund" was born. This law allows the EPA to clean up abandoned hazardous waste sites and to require responsible parties to perform cleanups or reimburse the government for EPA-led cleanups. For more than 30 years, the EPA has located and analyzed tens of thousands of hazardous waste sites, protected people and the environment from contamination at the worst sites, and involved communities in their cleanup.

The Brownfields Program awards three types of grants, but not all applicants or sites are eligible for certain grants.

funds that do not have to be repaid, to local governments to launch programs aimed at cleaning up the estimated 450,000 brownfields in existence so that the properties can be productive in the future.

In the early 1990s, the public's increasing interest in **sustainability** led the EPA to develop programs aimed at renewable sources of energy, such as the Green Power Partnership and Energy Star. The Green Power Partnership provides assistance and recognition to organizations that demonstrate environmental leadership by choosing "green" (efficient, nontoxic, and renewable) sources of energy. The EPA's Energy Star program—sometimes working with the U.S. Department of Energy—encourages companies to make their products more energy efficient to reduce fuel consumption. The development of renewable sources of energy is just one challenge the EPA faces as it leads the country into a more sustainable future.

Electric systems generated by both wind and solar can provide consistent power, no matter the weather conditions.

BRITISH ANTARCTIC SURVEY
Antarctica

In May 1985, British Antarctic Survey scientists shocked the world when they discovered a huge hole in the ozone layer—a blanket of air that blocks most of the sun's harmful ultraviolet rays from reaching the earth—over Antarctica. This led to a worldwide effort to ban the use of such chemicals as chlorofluorocarbons (CFCs), which were found to eat through the ozone. The ozone layer rebounded, and some scientists predicted that by 2080, global ozone would return to 1950s levels.

A Greener Future

Over the years, the EPA has set the standard for pollution control and environmental reform, but it will face even greater challenges in the future. Several scientific experts have noted that, despite the EPA's original function as legal enforcer, it has become an internationally respected leader in scientific research. Indeed, the EPA works with several agencies around the globe on issues from greenhouse gas emissions to climate change to global ecosystem monitoring.

The EPA is a member of the U.S. delegation to the United Nations' International Maritime Organization and its Marine Environment Protection Committee, which works to improve ship safety and prevent pollution from ships. The EPA advises on matters such as developing international standards for reducing exhaust and emissions and improving ships' energy efficiency. To promote energy-efficiency regulations (and products) worldwide, the EPA was a founding member of the Energy Star International Partnerships in 2010. The program puts consumer products such as appliances and electronics as well as new buildings through rigorous tests

Refuse that was once underwater may be exposed during severe droughts that claim even large reservoirs' supplies.

against strict energy-efficiency standards established by the EPA. Products earn the Energy Star label if they meet these energy requirements. All Energy Star products sold in member countries are held to the same requirements as the U.S. program.

As the world faces issues related to climate change, the EPA often leads America's response. Together with member nations of the international treaty known as the United Nations Framework Convention on Climate Change (UNFCCC), the EPA studies how human activities can be changed to prevent greenhouse gases from overtaking the atmosphere. When gases such as carbon dioxide, methane, nitrous oxide, and ozone are released into the atmosphere, they absorb and redirect the sun's warmth, increasing the greenhouse effect. Part of this radiation is aimed toward the earth's surface and the lower atmosphere, trapping heat. Without greenhouse gases, Earth's surface would be about 0 °F (-18 °C). With the gases, the average temperature is closer to 59 °F (15 °C). When the concentration of greenhouse gases is too high, though, the heat that is trapped within the atmosphere can cause the global temperature to rise

As the world faces issues related to climate change, the EPA often leads America's response.

gradually. This also affects sea levels, snow and ice melt, and other phenomena. The UNFCCC aims to help countries negotiate ways of reducing emissions of gases such as carbon dioxide to help lessen the effects of global warming.

The EPA also provides leadership in the Global Methane Initiative, a partnership of more than 20 nations dedicated to harnessing and repurposing methane from sources such as agriculture, coal mines, landfills, oil and gas systems, and municipal wastewater facilities. By reducing methane emissions, the Initiative also creates local jobs and sources of clean, alternative energy while improving air and water quality.

Worldwide population growth, the movement of people to new areas, and industrial expansion to **developing countries** present the EPA with new challenges of pollution and hazardous waste control. As more people make use of a limited supply of natural and man-made resources, ecosystems suffer the strain. An alarming amount of trash and waste is also created, and more pollution chokes the atmosphere. In recent years, electronic waste, or e-waste, has skyrocketed. Although recycling programs exist for electronics, plastics, and other

Mexico City's limited water supply is not enough for all 22 million of its residents, many of whom have no direct access to it.

The 700-mile-long (1,127 km) Brooks Range runs west to east through ANWR and other Alaskan wilderness.

waste products, the EPA is concerned that these materials too often end up in trash bins rather than places where they can be safely recycled. The increased use of electronic equipment in developing countries also presents concerns. According to the EPA, these countries do not have the necessary environmental standards in place or the authority to manage such environmental hazards.

The issue of opening up U.S. national parks and wildlife refuges to oil drilling and gas production has proven to be a hot topic for the EPA and other environmental groups, as well as with the politicians and companies who want to mine these lands. Nowhere has this issue been more evident than in Alaska's Arctic National Wildlife Refuge (ANWR). The 19.6-million-acre (7.9 million ha) wildlife sanctuary is home to millions of animals, including grizzly bears, wolves, foxes, caribou, whales, and birds. Beneath the **permafrost** is also potentially one of the U.S.'s richest supplies of oil. The 1980 law that created ANWR also provided for 1.5 million acres (607,000 ha) of the coastal plain to be kept available for potential gas and oil exploration, at

Congress's discretion. In 2005, Congress debated the issue but decided not to pass a bill that would have paved the way for such activity. As the U.S. continues to confront significant energy concerns in the future, the EPA will likely encounter increased pressure to make more federal lands and national parks available for resource development.

At the same time, the federal government and environmental groups push the EPA to take stronger actions to preserve the environment for future generations. In 2013, President Obama identified global climate change as one of the most important environmental issues facing the world. He outlined a plan to reduce carbon emissions from power plants, which account for about 40 percent of all U.S. greenhouse gas pollution. He asked the EPA to work closely with states and industries to establish standards that would result in the desired reductions. During Obama's first term as president (2009–13), the U.S. more than doubled its use of wind and solar energy. The EPA was tasked with continuing to develop and expand the use of such clean,

... the federal government and environmental groups push the EPA to take stronger actions to preserve the environment for future generations.

renewable sources of power.

In the past, critics have accused the EPA of not strictly defining what is considered a safe level for a certain chemical's impact on human health. This has led some companies to challenge the EPA's enforcement of those standards. For instance, the Clean Air Act requires a permit for sources that exceed either 100 or 250 tons (90.7 or 227 t) per year of a particular pollutant. However, the EPA concluded that enforcing this threshold for greenhouse gases would be impractical because millions of companies and people would need to be permitted. So the EPA decided to relax the threshold for greenhouse gases. Critics then accused the EPA of interpreting the Clean Air Act to give itself permission to change the law at will.

States and industries that experience economic hardship as a result of certain regulations imposed by the Clean Air Act also have harsh words for the EPA. The Clean Air Act was originally meant to be a cooperative effort between the federal government and the states in which the EPA set standards. However, states that have a significant number of people working in places such as coal mines and power plants often resist when the EPA raises its standards. They criticize the EPA for what they see as threats to people's

AGENCY INSIDER

GAYLORD NELSON

Wisconsin senator Gaylord Nelson was passionate about the environment. Inspired by student protests against the Vietnam War in 1969, he wanted to spur similar teach-ins about the environment. As a result, on April 22, 1970, the first Earth Day, 20 million Americans took to their streets, parks, and auditoriums to rally for a healthy, sustainable environment. Earth Day created momentum for further environmental actions such as the Clean Air Act, Clean Water Act, and Superfund, as well as the creation of the EPA.

ORD NELSON

Open-pit coal mining may be safer for the health of miners, but it is still a destructive force on the land.

survival and livelihoods. They argue the EPA targets chemicals that have little impact on the greenhouse effect but that cost a lot to enforce. In 2014, the U.S. Supreme Court heard several cases brought by industry groups and individual states. The court took a long time to decide whether the EPA's authority extended to regulating greenhouse gases under a permit program for stationary sources of pollution. A loss for the EPA could remove a whole category of pollutants (not just greenhouse gases) from the permit program, which required any new major polluting facility to obtain a permit before construction was completed.

In its relatively brief existence, the EPA has done much to broaden its influence around the globe. As the world changes and new environmental issues arise, the EPA will have to adjust its enforcement of pollution control standards. It will also face the task of working with organizations and governments in the U.S. and around the world to research and develop new technologies for renewable energy and clean resources. The stakes are high, as the EPA's future is inextricably linked with the very fate of the environment itself.

The Supreme Court has final say in how American agencies and individuals receive "equal justice under law."

NATIONAL ENVIRONMENTAL JUSTICE ADVISORY COUNCIL
Warren County, North Carolina, U.S.A.

In September 1982, the residents of Warren County, North Carolina, made headlines when they protested the dumping of toxic soil at a community landfill. Protesters argued that the state's decision to put a toxic waste dump there exploited area residents, who were mainly poor and African American. The incident helped to spur the environmental justice movement. In 1993, the National Environmental Justice Advisory Council, an EPA federal advisory committee, was established to ensure that environmental laws treat all people fairly, regardless of race or income.

GLOSSARY

acid rain rain that contains dangerous chemicals emitted from car and factory exhaust

biodiesel renewable, clean-burning diesel replacement that is made from resources such as agricultural oils, recycled cooking oil, and animal fats

bioremediation a waste management technique that uses organisms to break down hazardous substances into safe substances or to remove or neutralize pollutants from a contaminated site

conservation the protection or careful use of animals, plants, and natural resources to prevent them from being lost or wasted

developing countries the poorest nations, which are generally characterized by a lack of healthcare, nutrition, education, and industry; most developing countries are in Africa, Asia, and Latin America

ecology the science that deals with the relationships of living things to one another and to their environments

ecosystem a community of organisms that live together in an environment

fossil fuels fuels formed by decaying plants and animals over millions of years

greenhouse gas a gas that builds up in Earth's atmosphere and prevents the release of heat; examples include carbon dioxide and CFCs

hazardous waste an industrial byproduct that is destructive to the environment or dangerous to the health of people or animals

industrialization the process of having highly developed industries or manufacturing activities

mediation an attempt to reach a peaceful settlement or agreement between disputing parties

nuclear describing a form of energy produced when atoms are split or joined together

permafrost a layer of soil that is always frozen in very cold regions of the world

radioactive characteristic of substances such as uranium that give off particles of energy as their atoms decay; the energy can be dangerous to human health

smog fog or haze mixed with smoke and other air pollutants

statutes written laws formally created by a government

sustainability the quality of using a resource in such a way in which it is not depleted or permanently damaged

SELECTED BIBLIOGRAPHY

Collin, Robert W. *The Environmental Protection Agency: Cleaning Up America's Act.* Westport, Conn.: Greenwood Press, 2006.

Colten, Craig E., and Peter N. Skinner. *The Road to Love Canal: Managing Industrial Waste before EPA.* Austin: University of Texas Press, 1995.

INDEX